APPROACH TO MURANO

Jack Clemo was born in 1916 near St Austell, Cornwall. Son of a clay-kiln worker, he received only a village school education, but devoted himself entirely to writing throughout a restless adolescence. He remained a mystical recluse during his twenties, living in poverty with his widowed mother. By 1955 he had become deaf and blind.

His first published novel, *Wilding Graft*, won an Atlantic Award in Literature from Birmingham University in 1948. An allegorical novel, *The Shadowed Bed*, which he wrote soon afterwards, was eventually published in 1986 by Lion Publishing. He is the author of two volumes of autobiography, *Confession of a Rebel* (1949) and *Marriage of a Rebel* (1980), both recently reissued in paperback by Hodder, and a record of personal faith, *The Invading Gospel* (1958), reissued by Lakeland Books in 1972 and by Marshall and Pickering in 1986.

His first collection of poems, *The Clay Verge*, appeared in 1951, and was incorporated in a larger volume, *The Map of Clay*, ten years later. *The Wintry Priesthood*, a sequence which won an Arts Council Festival of Britain poetry prize in 1951, was also printed in *The Map of Clay*. Four other collections of poetry followed: *Cactus on Carmel* (1967), *The Echoing Tip* (1971), *Broad Autumn* (1975) and *A Different Drummer* (1986). His *Selected Poems* (Bloodaxe Books, 1988) was a Poetry Book Society Recommendation; his latest collection, *Approach to Murano*, was published by Bloodaxe in 1993. He has published two other books with Cornish imprints, *The Bouncing Hills*, humorous dialect stories and light verse (Truran Publications, Redruth, 1983), and *Banner Poems*, local descriptive pieces (Cornish Nationalist Publications, 1989). *Clay Cuts*, an illustrated limited edition of early clay-image poems, was published by Previous Parrot Press, Oxford, in 1992.

He was awarded a Civil List pension in 1961, and an honorary D.Litt degree from Exeter University in 1981. He married his wife Ruth in 1968, and in 1984 they left Cornwall and settled permanently in her home town of Weymouth in Dorset. Their courtship and marriage was the subject of a biography, *Clemo: A Love Story* by Sally Magnusson (Lion Publishing, 1986).

APPROACH TO MURANO

JACK CLEMO

BLOODAXE BOOKS

ISBN: 1 85224 192 6

First published 1993 by
Bloodaxe Books Ltd,
P.O. Box 1SN,
Newcastle upon Tyne NE99 1SN.

Bloodaxe Books Ltd acknowledges
the financial assistance of Northern Arts.

Cover printing by J. Thomson Colour Printers Ltd, Glasgow.

Printed in Great Britain by
Cromwell Press Ltd, Broughton Gifford, Melksham, Wiltshire.

For
BENEDICT AND LILAH RAMSDEN,
our guides in Venice,
with gratitude for a rare friendship.

Prefatory Note

Most of these poems were written in Weymouth, but I have included some of the last poems I composed amid the Cornish clay-tips before settling in Dorset in 1984. The geographical change was related to a spiritual and emotional shift away from cramped and austere concepts of truth, and the double movement made me receptive during visits to other parts of Britain and, even more significantly, to Venice. The city's glass-producing centre, the island of Murano, became a symbol of the clear-cut, luminous image, contrasting with my bleared and heavy clay idiom. The character-sketches in this collection, balancing the personal record, depict historical figures who were in my mind at times while I approached the Murano stage.

My thanks are due to the editors of the following journals in which many of the poems have been printed: *Acumen, Christian, Christian Woman, Cornish Banner, The Cut, Dorset Year Book, Nexus, Orbis, Outposts, Poetry Ireland, Resurgence, The Rialto, South West Review, Symphony* and *Westwords*. 'Meeting-points' first appeared in *Poems for Charles Causley*, edited by Michael Hanke (Enitharmon, 1982). 'The Kilns' was published in *New Christian Poetry*, edited by Alwyn Marriage (Collins, 1990).

'Open Waters', 'Jean-Pierre de Caussade' and 'Palazzo Rezzonico' are reprinted from my *Selected Poems* (Bloodaxe Books, 1988), and now restored to their original context in *Approach to Murano*.

Contents

PART ONE

11   The Model
12   Perennial
13   Meeting-points
14   At Cerne
15   Near the Race
16   Barbecue
17   The Split
19   Ironies of a Homecoming
20   On the Prospect of Leaving My Birthplace

PART TWO

22   Jonathan Swift: June 1723
24   Emily Brontë
25   Haworth Keys: 1840
26   Tryphena
27   William Barnes
28   John Harris

PART THREE

30   Link at Oxford
31   Windsor
32   Open Waters
33   Fleet
34   Mersey Tunnel
35   In Wales
36   Sortridge Manor
37   Abbotsbury Gardens

PART FOUR

40   Island Contrasts
41   St Margaret of Cortona
43   Reception
44   Pascal
45   Jean-Pierre de Caussade
46   Hudson Taylor to Maria
48   The Kilns
49   Dissenting Solo

PART FIVE

52　Sunset in Dorset
53　Emigrant
54　Frostbite
55　Keswick Revisited
56　Festal Magnet
57　Palazzo Rezzonico
58　Late Honeymoon
59　San Lazzaro
60　Venice
61　A Slant from St Mark's
62　Ring and Pen

PART ONE

The Model

Modestly harboured where my pen glides,
Near the uncut western Channel,
A Venetian souvenir glitters, high and apart –
A gondola, swan-smooth in Murano glass,
Gold-edged, recalling the guided waters.

It's my symbol of unsplintered clarity,
Perfected vision, owing nothing
To the blast-thuds of diseased rock,
Or the muddy, snarling iron tooth.
These Cornish images suggest the dull cup,
Not the entrancing voyage.

I may still use figures foreign to Venice,
Bleared in Irish mist, fighting Chinese dragons,
Lightning-blinded on English moors;
But there's a relevance, a wry bond,
A scar reflected from my love-pit grapple.
Such wounds were healed in Dorset and forgotten
In St Mark's: I crossed the Rialto
Choosing the unscathed lucid prow.

Beneath the bridge, while this miniature
Glass gondola was being bought,
The unique oar dipped and a multitude
Of heaven-trapped lovers' longings glowed again
In my maturing transit,
Within the clarity I offer now.

Perennial

Modern lights in Venice
Do not annul, or even distort,
Tradition's dowry. When the trespassing glow
Saps the haunting moon-flutter on St Mark's,
On quaint shops, canal craft, statues in squares,
The classic soul still breathes uncheapened.

At night-drop in English cities the fagged crowds
Sharpen in illusion, seeing the cold
Steady white wave teem with traffic,
But here no vehicle, no jolt of brakes,
Shakes the ancient road. There are only footsteps,
Footsteps and low voices: you think of lanterns
And torches bobbing a thousand years ago.

Fancy the relevant dream-drawn walkers'
Plod across bridges and islands
To a church rite or a lovers' rendezvous!
Modern light, falling on roads unbruised
By dubious transport, cannot distort,
Much less annul, our primal trysts.

Meeting-points
(for Charles Causley)

He burst into my pit-land, grit-land,
Before I turned from it towards the sea,
And his flying images have spanned
The continents, wholesome as that broad greeting.
Frolic of rhyme from cruising fancies,
Or the snatch of a carved, compassionate memory:
Slum delinquents, a grim moor-backed killing;
Ship's roll in soft Pacific tremors
Suddenly trounced by guns; or he's pitching
Today's pew and schoolroom through a breeze of antiquity.

And now I lounge at Aggie Weston's
Near his birthday, near grinding Chesil.
Sailors play darts, ask a gospeller questions,
Rest their bare feet and sing.
I think of his shore leave, the mind's homeward voyage,
The thrust through wordy torrents until
The apt phrase was shaped and shining.
I can fancy the poet's hand
As close as when it passed me the ring
In the grey light of a Cornish chapel.

At Cerne

What's Hercules doing here,
Deep in our Dorset chalk?
Above streets where shriven pilgrims used to walk
The hill vibrates with fear.

Clash the wicket-gate, approach the fence,
Straddle the high stile:
You are gripped by Roman hearts in exile,
Their hate and ache still tense

In the scars they left, the indelible wounding
Of this conquered curve of land.
They must see their hero-god at hand
When they took a slave-girl, a battle's pounding.

And so, with British wild tusked boars
Goring nearby, the Giant was shaped,
A myth transplanted, grim and undraped,
From soft Mediterranean shores.

Cows wander here now, but cannot tame
The pagan bristle, the poised horn;
The hacked earth's protest must be borne –
The sunken ashes, sacrificial flame.

This heath-slope, raped in the dark search
For ritual power, can be surveyed
As a curious relic or a scrawl made
Modern by a culture's lapse and smirch.

Between hill and valley – between the crude
Ruthless image and the shrines
Of cloistered prayer – I feel our sign's
Framed within wedlock, blood's beatitude.

I shall leave Cerne with its two spheres
Spun fine in me through your tracing –
Both pressures erased, your laughter gracing
The innocent tea-shop, ending fears.

Near the Race

The stoical, mesmerised boatman,
Scanning the boil and claw of that sea-trap,
Would not even take famous ashes
To sow peace close to the cauldron.

Serene trust is possible
Only on solid ground, like this rib of Portland –
Old as the Roman rod, yet towering
At a safe span from today's nag and drag
Of confused waters battling for harbour.

I sense the hiss and turmoil
Of ideologies, speculations, doubts,
Now rampant; and I would not venture
Too near the ferment of enquiry.

To think the Nicene way
In the midst of nuclear tension
And the secular advance
Seems monstrous to some whose craft
Flirts with the whirlpool.

I stay firmly on the rock
And breathe the Nicene marvels every day.
I adapt to quick tempo and method
On isle or mainland: surface health
Is finer than morbid depth in the faithful.

Let the pop gospel vibrate over dry limestone –
At least it means you're not drowned.
But I don't fancy
Any bone of my belief
Lying abreast of a bishop's on the sea-bed.

The Race is a treacherous whirlpool off Portland Bill, Dorset.

Barbecue

Sparks nuzzle nimbly into crevices,
Losing their glow between the dry salt stones;
The picnic fire kindles apace,
Pungent and smoke-frilled, out-colouring the tones
Of a bemused sunset. This is Chesil
At a homely and passive hour,
With a group of joyous, unmolesting figures
Squatting on the slanted pebble-face,
In harmony with the tranquil
Play of the tide-tip a little lower,
Where a solitary child is bathing,
Waving, laughing as she looks
At the clear base of flame, near which some women attend
To potatoes and sausages, adroit as gypsy cooks.

Song-sheets flutter
And are laid down in the fading daylight;
Shadowy arms poise a guitar.
The blended singing voices
Leap softly through the fire's splutter
And the sea's combing thrum.

Hymn-snatches hint at an opening
For the adventurous spirit; the gathering night
Breathes in a marginal mystery, soul and atom
Fused in a purged haunting music of desire.
The child leaves the water, climbs unafraid
To her chanting comrades and the supper-roasting fire.

The Split

Past Upwey and curving round
Westward along the Bridport road,
The sea showing a blue cheek
Beyond the clogged tongue of Chesil
I muse in a purring red car,
Uncertain where my roots are.

Am I leaving home or homeward bound?
Where the car starts or drops its load
My wife makes a world authentic;
There's paradox – the poet rebel
Tidies the lawn and flicks a duster
Around some private furniture.

Two lives nurtured far apart
Bear the summer's dismantling toss
To and fro, across three county borders –
Released yet strained by rival orders.

The pang as the locked house vanishes, the long
Cessation of contacts grown familiar,
The attempt to adjust, exchange
That friend for this, this church for that,
Weighing the gain and loss
At both ends. Our marriage must shine
Equally at each end, but which is mine?

Am I most integral
In the flounce of clay-dust or the slap of sea-brine?
Do I miss my Cornish granite wall
More than the Portland stone the postman pressed,
Pushing my love-letters through a Dorset door-slot?
Are the hints of comfort keenest
On the urban balcony or the cottage stairs?

Must I choose Wessex fixtures
As permanent touchstones of the inmost hearth
Or bear to the last rooting curve
This toss of the hub to and fro?

I am not one of the questioners
Baffled by a source turned hollow:
My wife shares the car's swerve,
Near Bridport now and heading
Past sheepfolds to the neutral red Devon earth.

Ironies of a Homecoming

'Clay-tips again!' Always the same words
At the same point on my homeward journey,
South of Bodmin, turning to reach Bugle.
It is here that the strangeness starts:
Having sea-spelled Dorset months behind me,
I no longer understand
The gaunt hills' lines of struggle.

After four hours' travel
From the snug road at Rodwell,
Which I have crossed a hundred times,
Secure with my wife or hand-in-hand
With a bubbly sun-sprayed friend,
I feel the shade of a fortress,
A military stiffness, wounded contours.

Memories revive: the pits' hiss and blast;
Hail of gale-torn dune-crust;
Narrow plank bridges over gullies;
Rail-ridged sidewalks of hot kilns,
Almost dark, the wooden awnings down,
And no windows in the blind sullen walls.

It is not to these blighting metaphors
That my heart returns, but only
To the screened and exempt pasture
Of one small cottage
Where Cornish sprays of friendship
Gather around a Weymouth flower.

On the Prospect of Leaving My Birthplace

Don't talk of my being uprooted
From the clay-beds of my childhood:
The man baptised, reborn, has no little father
Projecting him from a mould of infancy.
The boy could watch the white twisted fingers
Casting grim spells outside the cottage window
And be duly absorbed. I can't.

My roots are in my soul's Jerusalem,
Which has appeared in many forms
Of the warmed heart: Wimpole Street, Aldersgate Street,
Spurgeon's Tabernacle, Bernadette's shrine,
The Brownings' Florence and Barth's Safenwil.
How could the sick, fear-dazed child
At Goonamarris know of these?
Pit-blasts could not unearth the key
To my real self, the pilgrim-planted
Treasures of redemptive memory.

Clay-ravage was a fitting stage
For the doomed creature I seemed to my young mother,
Not for the happy husband I am to my wife,
Serene in mind and flesh, busily blending
Those foreign voices that broke the twisted clay-spell.

For nearly seventy years the slate roof
Has slanted above my sleep or my empty bed,
But the man I am, the fulfilled believer,
Needs palms, sweet modest hills and gentle
Cleansing ripples on the unhacked beach,
Not the rubble-wreckage of defiled meadows,
Or the iron teeth of an outgrown rejected cradle.

PART TWO

Dorset Roots

East Woodnates and East Stour:
Two regions where ambiguous seed-plots
Knotted into history, shaping a subtle power
That gripped a multitude through the penned word.

Woodnates nurtured the Browning family
Centuries back – the broad view,
Culture, mellow hills and hideous wealth
Piled from a sweltering plantation
Remote on St Kitts, where half-starved negro women
Shrieked and fainted under the whip
While a Mistress Browning sought calm fellowship,
Prim in her pew, swelling the church collection.

The poet's father turned from the sick trade,
Risked ruin that slaves might be free,
And though the poet's ringing voice
(Last heard in liberated Venice)
Never stirred Dorset air, his ancestry,
Growing tense elsewhere, marked his strident tones.

There was Fielding too, the favourite author
Of the poet's grandfather.
Unpruned luxuriant valleys of a river
Moulded his youth. The Stour's flow
Was fouled by brutish peasants, its jungle-dark bends
Choked with garbage, rotten rags and bones,
Sometimes a drowned girl, scandal-bruised.

Young Fielding heard coarse tavern songs,
Saw poachers brawl, yet clung to classic beauty,
Haunted by the grace at Lyme Regis,
The heiress he almost won. The two threads fused,
Grew to the massive sinews of *Tom Jones*.

Jonathan Swift: June 1723

In the gilded Dublin salons
Society shows its amused, witty talons,
And the Dean of St Patrick's is in flight.
He rides south towards Cork, alone,
The venom raging in his veins
With a haggard newness, scandal-blown.

He has been scarred often, storming through general silt –
Injustice, tyranny, Ireland's plight.
Bishops are acquiescent: he must fight,
Shoot satire from a clouding brain;
And now the heart's brawl of pride and guilt
Whirls fiercely under the arched female trap.

Vanessa is dead, and she died hating him
Because of that letter, her last and vain
Thrust, and his scorn-barbed snap
As he flung it back at her. Women at strife
For his sour, drained carcase: he had chosen one.
Stella had breathed the fatal words:
'She asks if I am your wife.'

Escape! But the low hills look grim;
Foul-smelling bogs, jagged rocks, ramshackle cabins,
And the stumbling skeletons,
The ragged, thieving Irish peasantry,
Repel him. There seems no remedy:
He has fumed and stung: the oppressors merely smile:
'He'll whip himself to madness, like his uncle.
Insanity behind him, he shuns marriage:
What triumphs can he get?'

The fugitive rides faster, his twisted visage
Bowed in the unpitying sunset.

Emily Brontë

Blend of heliotrope
And pink in heather on Penistone;
Alert grace of hares racing
To the shade of gnarled thorn or almond;
Above her the sweet beseeching
Carol of peewit and lark.

She lies scorched alone,
Fevered by nightmare traffic:
Roe Head, Law Hill, Brussels,
To the Cornish aunt's wild tales
Of fairies and dark magic
On Penwith moors, lonely and bold as these,
With Land's End near, the cleansing sea,
The Wolf's bright scribble of warning,
Then soft-spoken romantic isles.

But she aches for sullen winter,
Desolation of Haworth in a snow cell,
The crazed nun's vigil
Beside frozen bones
Until a bruised ecstasy
Tears open the unsmiling heaven.

Haworth Keys, 1840

The young white seamew, a gale's victim,
Harried inland to stony Haworth,
Wavered above the black waves of heather,
Hearing the whistle of wrecked thorns.

The practised native plover,
Riding its storm-tongued climate, darted low,
Close to the church wall, heard strange music:
Moor-Sybil at the damp discordant organ,
Plucking a hymn-tune, making the Sabbath-spell
Rise in a rasp of village voices.

Both birds, the fugitive, the homegoer,
Sped on, leaving to us the riddle
Of that ambiguous player – dutiful,
Rebellious, haunted on her dark border.

Tryphena

She stole from moon-softened Puddletown
And the little river smelling of inn-rinsings,
Took the heath-track towards Stinsford: green or brown,
The wild massed foliage pleased her.
She sang Dorset love-songs while the snakes hissed,
Called a blithe quip to a stumbling heath-cropper.

Breezy always, she had no fear of stings
From adders or fate. There was magic at Rushy Pool
Or on Rainbarrow: these furtive meetings
With her haunted, mysterious cousin
Had the rippling flavour of smuggled things.

As we watch, she is lost to us
In a shuffling fog of rumour,
Contending whispers and amorphous
Echoes and distortions. We glimpse the pair
Next at Weymouth, years later, and the ring's
Given before a storm breaks and sunders.

Prim gates at Coryates and Stockwell,
And her Plymouth post, headmistress of a school,
Shine to efface the smeared libel
Of the breeding dregs and a betrayal,
Puddletown pattern, outcast in the stained river.

We know a Gale blew her from Hardy's spell;
Bockhampton sealed Emma for the scarred grey height.
But whether the eclipsed, dark-tressed Tryphena
Escaped or was cheated, we would trust her memories
Of the pure enchanted heath in moonlight.

William Barnes

Homely and benign, the key moment,
Yet profound and startling too,
When a charming bundle of blue
Left the stage-coach at Dorchester,
Watched by obscure and pensive Barnes.

The once frail boy from Blackmore
Felt a wholeness glow in her:
It mounted to the vows, the tether
Of a heaven-blessed family.
They were to shape a quiet course
From Mere to the Frome-bordered town
And the ritual base at Whitcombe, under blue skies
Reflected in his carved, sturdy verse.

Gentle humour and warm humanity
Infused his growing skill as a craftsman.
Rural Dorset cast her vernacular
Wide and authentic through her son,
Who etched dream and grief or the sheer solace
Of common love and labour
In a thick, rounded landscape of peace.

He built until the beloved image fell
And faith's rock broadened for the widower.
Though the scholar-bard was stripped,
Serene trust shone in his lonely script
Penned in Came rectory, and lit the new scene –
Heath, woodland, sheepfold, the chiming bells'
Tap on the thatch-crowned routine
Of pleasure and pang in simple villagers.

He saw a studious young friend shorn
In the city's agnostic climate,
Heading for the blizzard at Max Gate
Even while seated in Winterbourne church,
Hearing the rector's sermon and the forlorn
Cawing of rooks in the graveyard.

A few more utterances and the strong
Aged voice was silenced, but unlike his friend's
Coldly-planned house, his rectory
Bloomed bold beyond his tomb-cross in a summer of song.

John Harris

Rattling through the pell-mell air
Down Dolcoath shaft, the lonely miner
Guided the inner tools of his craft.
A caged line jerked to a standstill
On the mind's hot branching bed,
Awaiting the blackberry juice,
Ink-substitute, the red scrawl on paper,
Or on his hat or fingernail,
Which would seal for us his incongruous treasure.

The golden phrase scooped in the tin seam
Must be the man's excuse
For a silent withdrawal, akin to prayer,
A lost look in the gentle eyes,
Half aroused from dream,
Bewildered, tenacious, hinting at soul-struggle
As he crouched and strained in the foul, flayed dust
Amid curse and spittle of a brute partner
And the lamp-flare's distorting thrust.

Holier here than in Burns or Clare,
The peasant fibre kindled by poetry.
Chaste and sober, faithful in Wesley's fold,
He grew as saint and rhymer,
His mine-sharpened vision, Bible drill,
Chiming with Billy Bray's praise, though fed
In a richer and subtler gallery.
He hymned the shy sweetheart's touch and hold,
And the wild flower's pure scent,
Raising among the Redruth slag-tips
An unstained simple testament.

PART THREE

Link at Oxford

I stepped out of Magdalen: the Lewis aura
Was heavy in corridors and jovial
In the breezy elegance of spires.
Shiver of limp leaves on college paths
Meant only that a season was doing its chores,
Irrelevant to the faithful. The bright bells
Would tingle along mental currents
More timeless than the Cherwell's.

I had intruded from an uncouth region,
A way of learning unknown to students
Who muse in the refined air
Of Addison's walk. I was there
On a holiday trip, untroubled
By syllabus, fees, examination systems,
The seethe of ordered thinking
Within the pattern of a don's lecture.

No such tradition or taste
Marked my early striving amid odours
Of clay chemicals and rusty scrap.
I saw tip-waggons bombard earth's beauty
Till my faith caught their mood – a hard working-class
Bulldozing, but untouched by the skilled Marxist,
The sceptical debater, the aesthete;
And the later wisdom, the grasp of loveliness,
Came otherwise than in a college room.

My harvest, too, is in libraries,
But rough-edged, elemental, prompted
By the long caress, the brief withdrawal,
Divine or feminine, never academic.
I am awed by the gulf, the two spheres –
Lewis's here, mine (some critics tell me)
Nearer to Bunyan's fens – converging,
Naming wholeness in a sick climate.

Fleet

The innocent young hand leads me
From the base of Butter Street,
And history tingles again in cold December.
I touch a rough pillar of Fleet,
The intact portion, its polished wood,
Metal-work, cloth coverings.
Her hand guides mine: this is a place of guidance
Even now, and so calm, I can scarcely
Picture the flood-swirl, mad to dismember
The outpost church. Inside surviving walls
Praise is secure, and rich dramatic colour.

Always the contrast: tides repressed
Or brawling like smugglers around the lagoon;
Snicker or scream of Chesil strand's
Long store of missiles; clump and garden
Bare or too rash with foliage;
And here, in this devout nest, the spell
Of an unchanging spirit, a boon
Immune from fickle seasons.

A pity for the lawless ones,
The wreckers, grim in our traditions.
We can fancy the shambling footfalls
Furtive in the dank tunnel –
Men bearing kegs or other loot
From Chesil to some vault, perhaps within reach
Of the midnight carol, the sound
Of the chanted mercy. Not a trace
Of guilt here: those dubious errands
Dissolve in a bright flood
And the treasure of innocent hands.

Open Waters

A slap of spray on my left ear
Makes me rub salt drops off my neck
And feel proud of my drenched collar.
The motor-launch quivers and tilts
At the heavier wave-banks. I lean overboard,
Pull a rope, shift with the unrhythmic roll,
Glad I've never been seasick,
And hardly attuned to an awareness
That I live in a sick world.

The pleasure-boat noses near
Warships, helicopters, the bleak naval base;
Portland prison squats glum on the cliff.
But our innocent craft, moored elsewhere
Last night, chugs safe and unshadowed.

Weather experts have told us
We breathe poisoned air – some nuclear leak.
I hazily take it – the snag
Of a warped breed's invention;
But this gusty wind, if poisoned, still feels fine,
And my wife laughs, forgetting the warning.

I think of another dimension –
A Dissent hub on a Weymouth quay,
An open baptistry, wet hair on my cheek;
And I touch the unquenched praise
Believers have always smuggled
Into a world ever menaced, yet intact.

Leaks of evil brought those convicts
To the drab rot of the cells;
Battleships scar our view of Sandsfoot
Because of poisoned politics.
But our pleasure-boat still dances
Like the affirming heart, the outreach
From the hymn-tongued immersion, till this leaking spray
Links me with the exempt waters.

Windsor

I plodded around Windsor Castle,
Of all places – I who was born
Under crusts of a drab trade, smoke-skewered,
Clammy with kiln-steam. But I had matured
Beyond the pit's smear of class prejudice.
I felt no sick proletarian scorn
For the massive grandeur: it impressed me
With hints of a divine rule, the ripple
Of the calm Thames a symbol of timeless flowing
Freedom beneath turrets and arches.

We were no gadding tourists,
My wife and I: she mused as she held my arm,
Guiding me past the guards, up the twists
Of ancient stairs, through flashes of warm
Sunshine. I touched the legacy:
Armour, art treasures, tapestry,
Padded walls and royal tombs,
The chapel where distant winds fanned faith,
Since queens had prayed there, fearful of rooms
Narrowed for birth or death.

The normal spread of luxury
Seemed wholesome – not a waste,
But a call to the full meaning
Of the shabbiest hour when, in poverty,
I had caught the ripe gleam, a foretaste
Of infinite wealth. I glimpsed my service,
Blessed the opulent, as a mystic may;
And in the castle I traced
The aura which had brought me singing
From clay-blight to a broad regal bay.

Mersey Tunnel

Quashed daylight, but we must be patient,
Think of the rocking keels above us,
Clatter of Merseyside, oil spreading,
Funnel and lumbering river,
Loaded cargo and the deep bed-pressure
On the solid arch that guards our serene car.
Does the little girl imagine fish?
It's an apt symbol, for this is Christmas,
The submerged moment in the cavern.

We're steering towards a vicarage, having touched
Roots, precious to us, at Birkenhead,
Birthplace of the sweet fish-dreamer.
Her dancing eyes await the bright shoals
Of Liverpool shops, toy-decked,
Holly beyond the common cargo,
And then the mystery in the vicarage
Epilogue before supper. There she'll keep
My hand on her tambourine and the swing
Of the high carol will mean heavenly traffic
No sorrow's sullen flood can reach.

In Wales
(for Catherine and Tracy)

I breathed at last on Welsh soil,
The larger Celtic strip, but felt unclaimed,
Intruding with my wife and two schoolgirls.
The northern air was keener than Cornish,
Rowans and mountains sagged in foreign light;
Even the cottages looked tense, trapped and secretive,
Warned by a recent earth-tremor.

We hummed and bounced safely enough
Across the long fantastic Runcorn Bridge,
Having packed our lunch on Merseyside.
I thought of Saltash, the sudden shock
Of exotic names on signposts, no more English.
The place-names here were weirder, soft and poignant,
Needing the harp, the throb of incantation,
But I knew the root, the racial trauma
Branded amid gorse, as at Liskeard.

We step out now from a caravan;
The wild land breathes, less solemn.
The girls climb higher, laughing in sun-teased grass:
No quake of ground or heart disturbs us.

We have sipped cordials where an earth-stroke fumbled:
Not a feature is split, not a casual
Glass on a wooden wall. This is believers' country
Mirrored for me: I grasp the symbol only
And am a native. The unread language
Stands firm on the white fingers.
I can guess its meaning, having proof
That this hour's pitch is authentic.

Sortridge Manor
(for the Ramsdens)

Near Tamarside, near modern girders
Upholding a safe road above the waters,
I recall the ancient crossing,
Slow ferry rattling through contrary tides,
Lights on at nightfall, the taste of danger,
Snapped links, the whole craft lost and drifting.

We are miles inside Devon, but the symbols grip me
Where a sturdy arch of medieval stone
Leads to a manor and the wrecked tracks
Of some fugitive, shepherded dreamers.

Young healthy girls greet me as usual
In the gravel drive, also our friend the priest.
We enter, leaving the rain of an Epiphany;
The girls show me a carved manger.

We shall confront strange territory soon,
Twilight masking the snap of a straight way,
Confusion in the timid or desperate hands
Touching ours with a hunger for acceptance.

The girls will go out to feed the sheep
Sheltered near the medieval crossing,
And the marooned souls, seeking freedom, will also feast,
Sensing ferry or bridge in our greeting,
Security in our caring hearts.

*Sortridge Manor, near Plymouth, is a centre
of domestic therapy for schizophrenics.*

Abbotsbury Gardens
(for Lucy and Susan)

In this cupped and sun-rinsed culture,
This sprawled dry foam of scented brilliance,
Invasion is the keynote, but it's friendly.
To me the hours pass in a zigzag
Of rough tracks, with step-flights, quaking bridges
Over a stream which chatters of English chalk
Even where tropical trees spear high and cast shadows
On our familiar grass and the smooth
Surprising bulk of a nested cannon
On which I sat for a minute.

I could picture the stately, long-vanished castle
Gripping the bluff-top, and the robed countess
In her trained garden that lolled this way
Towards an untidy wood. She scanned the sea
Or bent to a musk-rose, musing of husband-lore.

My wife explores the present wealth in freedom,
Buying a plant or booklet as a souvenir,
Or drinking the hues of a strutting peacock.
I am being guided and teased
By two girls bounced from distant Halesowen,
On holiday here – another invasion.

I can fancy a black-skinned Congo girl,
Child-wife of a pigmy, staring at bamboo,
Or a dainty, slant-eyed, yellow-faced
Japanese maiden fondling such blooms
As thrive here now, braving our northern climate.

Camellias and hydrangeas brush my cheek;
A girl lays my fingers gently
On tufts of shag, like coconut fibre
But thick as her hair, encircling a palm-trunk.
Pungent mint is held to my nostrils;
A hard, notched, wind-tumbled cone taps my hand.

The small Halesowen dog leaps vainly
At pheasants flying above the foreign growths.
They have a broad view of the pulsing Channel
And the sweet protective inland hills
Rich in history, rich in legends of invasion.
The birds are fearless; their nests are safe:
The keynote is still peace.

PART FOUR

Island Contrasts

Cypress groves of San Michele
Stand plumed and ceremonial,
Their shadows massive, soothing the mourners,
For this is the burial island
To which even gondolas creep heavily,
Laden as funeral barges.

The distant casino, the Lido fever,
Seem trite and unworthy here,
But not the soaring campanile
Pouring the bells' 'Gloria'
On the treasures of unwidowed Venice.

Neither ignoble nor tawdry
Is the historic image
Of the Doge in his sturdy vessel,
Sober as a grave-side priest,
Yet chanting nuptials on Ascension Day:
'*Mare, noi to sposiamo...*'
'We wed thee, O sea...'

The symbol broadens: travellers pass San Michele,
Nearing Murano's sea of glass
Spread from a craftsman's fount, ungrieving
In its crisp and festal welcome.

St Margaret of Cortona

(1249-1297)

In that fierce age of Flagellants,
Of Francis's stigmata and wars about relics,
Peasant-wild Margaret built the natural scandal
At Laviano, seared by no conscience-pricks,
Wanton at twelve. If she looked towards Alverno
It was for a horseman or woodcutter she could woo.

The olives ripened in Tuscan valleys,
And Margaret was fruitful but did not wed.
She crossed the hills and joined the castle servants
Of a young noble, and soon his bed
Made her a lady, then a slave: she was mistress
And mother, cramped by this passion's press.

The hound whined at the castle gate,
Slunk starved and ominous to Margaret's room.
She followed it back to the forest,
Where new-cut faggots made a flimsy tomb
For her murdered lover. Revenge of a rival
Ended her reign, her riches, beauty and all.

The way of penance next, the body-hatred,
Her old reckless folly and public show
Twisted by guilt. She had seen half-naked women
Scourge themselves in the streets: she would go
Beyond them to expiate her shame.
Out of Franciscan shelter she burst, a disfigured flame.

In the haunts of her florid coquetries
She was led by a neck-noose, the blood dripping
Over her rags as she screamed confessions
Proper for Magdalenes. Here was soul-stripping,
A wrestle for pardon and the saint's crown
As viewed in hot mists, faith's twilight zone.

Our savage century may yield parallels
When the choked spirit erupts. She was blessed
With visions, mystic gifts...Yet all's distorted.
Did Christ bid Mary mutilate her breast,
Scar the ministering lips, or win
His love through a rope's chafe on her chin?

Reception
(Pope John-Paul II: May-June 1982)

Under Cornish slate, piously grey,
Nonconformist, a golden ray
Spreads from basilicas. My desk vibrates
With the triumphant song that consummates
The domed smile. Some ancient warp
Is healed or suspended: there's a welcoming harp
In Knox's citadel, and the deep strains
Of our 'Cwm Rhondda' hallow the plane's
Lift in farewell towards the Roman sky.

My roof stays simple, close to Billy Bray,
But I called him a St Francis, and I share,
In this half-foreign light, the rare
Heart's leap where crossed Whit winds have blown.
Our nuclear-threatened desert, a world unknown
To Knox and Bray, has spurred
The sunny clasp, the joyous clapping heard
Here, making my cottage tingle
Amid the aloof clay, the forgotten brambly dingle.

Pascal

He graciously thinned his library, a rare act
   For a scholar, dying with only two
Books in his home: nun-sister,
   No wife, matched the ascetic martyrdom.

Paradox also, and a challenge to us
   Still, this cultural strip-tease:
It must, at least, have amused the angels
   Who guarded the *Pensées*, the future feast.

He jettisoned the wide shimmer
   Of the pundit's pickled guess,
The classic tag, the tripping guide,
   The heretic's braying brag.

No tools for the stuffy building,
   No craft for the sorting out:
He died bare and joyful, at the unslanted source –
   Heaven's Word and the Hippo chronicle.

Jean-Pierre de Caussade

He went blind at seventy or so,
Groped for candles and the holy cup
In the bristling Jesuit house
He had guided firmly at Toulouse;
And no one guessed that his eyes once led a quill
On lengthy excursions in a cramped cell
To reap his pale, prayer-battered insights.
His book remained anonymous
For a century, feeding a mystic flow
In his confrères and some Quietists.

Age and the quenched rainbow set me
Near him, but my human probe
Flared far from his placid theory
About an equal influx of divine love
At every moment, making the present impact
The only one now valid and heaven-charged.
Rather, grace soothes my opaque flats of fact,
During the test-hour, from past heights
Of the senses' sunniest ardour.

We poets seldom shine at contemplation
Or monkish meditation:
I am rare, for I stress prayer
And, like Jean-Pierre, know the purged soul's delights,
But the ties, the tides, the tidings do not tally.
The ascetic hint from uncomfortable mists
Seems a scurrilous thorn to me, chiding my praise
For a secure day's
Teeming caress and the sea-foam on her hair.

Hudson Taylor to Maria

Chinese yellow tinged the Barnsley sunrise:
My father's little chemist's shop smelled
Of Western hygiene: big clogs clacked on the cobbled street.
I dreamed of pigtails, tiny deformed feet,
Mandarins, coolies. My weak eyes
Saw that the sky was English and I rebelled.

Why the heart-cry for China when our moors
Were full of black magic, our town yards
Foul almost as Ningpo slums? I wanted a white wife:
Two Yorkshire girls loved me and clung, made strife
Deep in me: their love, unlike yours,
Was grooved in domestic smugness, prim safeguards.

Malayan heats toned your first soft longings:
Whole hemispheres apart, we somehow
Shared the yellow magnet. I sailed alone for Shanghai,
While orphan pangs pitched you to the near-by
Treaty port where I found you: heart-strings
Wound shyly, then gripped fiercely in cold shadow.

We nearly wrecked the mission: we had seen
Asia's need where its sewer-hungers gape
And girls just bought for brothels scream, beaten half the night
Till they consent. Our warm bond not polite,
Demure or prudent, had to mean,
Headlong as redemption, a breach of the set shape.

I was left with no salary, no church:
We married in blind faith, pioneers,
Defying a furious bishop. But the Chinese watched,
Curious about our God. Our trials unlatched
Doors barred to snug preachers: the search
Of a few drugged souls was halted despite the jeers.

Yes, we have blazed a trail, knocked deep inland:
Our love beat stronger than temple gongs;
Our children's eyes danced, fearless of the carved dragons' teeth.
Some flower of wisdom has burst from its sheath:
Barnsley, Penang...twin points expand,
Meet in our marriage, challenge China's wrongs.

*Hudson Taylor was the first Protestant missionary to penetrate
inland China. He was also remarkable for his romantic marriage,
achieved in spite of fierce opposition from the girl's guardian.*

The Kilns
(to C.S. Lewis)

A rambling house where academic talk
Once buzzed and your pen stung Screwtape
And honey flowed when a foreign tongue,
Witty with your faith, unsealed a bliss
Deeper than logic. The odd bond sweetened,
Breathed Grecian air, then found Greek tragedy,
Fate's waspish venom. Joy limped up these stairs
And a final anguish shook the walls
Free from legends of a dry scholar.

I feel the scorching irony
In this quiet room as I stroke the hollow
Your shifting bulk wore in a big arm-chair.
The house-name prods faint images
Of my Cornish gut: hot kiln, steam, bubbling clay,
Thick suffocating dust that muffled rails
Where a tank-waggon vomited. It's a way
Of refining: some such jargon
I recall dimly. Not a trace
Of its truth in my wedded life. I salute
Your faith's hard test, but I am past my furnace.

I admire the autumn garden
Which you blessed with her in timeless moments,
The bees around the flowers, hurting no-one;
And you turned back indoors to a feast, a foretaste,
The wine among spilled books by firelight,
Your dream-track reaching to unflawed planets,
Your fancies solid in her puckish creed.

Here were the springs that fed me,
Parched for hope amid sullen kilns;
And the present bounty, my wife's hand
Guiding me to your door,
Assures me that your blithe wisdom
Rides now unwounded: Joy still hunts
For surprises, teasing after the grave sting.

Dissenting Solo

I know what Matthew Arnold droned
   About old age, but not for me
The whine of waning pagan pride,
   Agnostic nullity.

All that brings bliss is still alert
   Within my nerves at sixty-eight;
My spirit rules to counteract
   The sad reflective state.

I who was never young in youth
   Now taste unjaded nuptial thrills,
Sharpened inside the weathered grace
   Of creeds and canticles.

I'm truant, yet my lines run straight,
   Disquietingly orthodox:
The raffish fashions of the arts
   Are not my favourite shocks.

Why do these shuffling poets spit
   Derision at faith's rosy clues,
And glumly boost their nettled night
   To prompt the slick reviews?

Firm, clear-edged as Murano-ware,
   My memories flash the eternal wink;
The Last Trump's merry in my blood
   While cultures reel or blink.

Dismay and doubt in haggard stone
   The time-bound crust of nature yields;
But I played truant: even my kiss
   Echoed in mystic fields.

My song's undrained because I strum
   Baptised and sense-researching keys
No poets touch till Mary's Son
   Annuls their sanctities.

Those wailing sanctities include
    Homeric dirge and 'Dover Beach':
Noble enough. My honest art
    Prefers the exultant breach.

PART FIVE

Sunset in Dorset

This smooth ripe landscape of humility,
This county without a city,
Without a cathedral to take religion
Stonily skyward – it's an epitome
Of my retrieved life and my terminal home.

On the arid and arrogant plateau,
In lulls of the clay-storm, I knew
Grace had assailed the tragic peaks
To liberate the captive, move me on
To a valley of peace and unflawed beauty.

I have lost the tense, suffering sinew,
The thunderous quake, the twisted view
Between smoke-darkened stacks; and who,
Caring for truth, would regret the transition?

I have not lapsed flaccidly
Into trite evasions of the iron creed,
Nor fed a migrating spirit with the fancied
Insipid flowers in the natural dell.
Still complex in stroking sunset,
I feel my first faith, loyal and rewarded.

Let me abide now, the apt
Images around me – Cerne-sober or capped
With carnival at our watering-place.
The uncrusted life is lapped
By a grace in human pressures
Where tucked tides lift an ancient secret
To the domestic garden, and a teasing sparkle
Flits in young corners of the harbour chapel.

Emigrant

Mine is a life which, youthward, was caught
In the cosmic coil, dragged deep
Through anguished currents, choked with questioning.
The sharks' teeth, piercing the weedy tangle,
Stripped much, threatened all. Faith saved me – yes, but pent
On a clay ledge barren in storm,
And, alone there, I mused starkly
On what the cruel coil meant
And what the hacking thunder taught.

But now it's incredible: climate and setting
Are reversed in my riper thought.
No gale howls here, roses are nodding red;
There's blue sky above every warm road
That leads to my feasts: no fight for a foothold!
I believe, no longer darkly
Despite God's silence and frown, but because
The whisper came and the smile spread,
And, much surprised, I am awed by His pampering.

Frostbite

Siberian ice-blast, in a freak prowl,
Tested the roots in English soil.
It struck, that grim, snow-masked,
Silent assassin, at Sandsfoot. Where we basked,
Hands on the regal and embossed
Warm palm-trunk, only an earth-scar
Speaks: our tropical treasure fought and lost.

The products of two hemispheres,
Both foreign to us, clashed on this cliff,
And when the white smother melted
From the still-breathing roses, we saw the green spears
Of the palm-trees, made for hot sandstorm war,
Fade and droop as the sap dried stiff.

A rare grace has slipped from these sea-lapped Gardens:
Some would be negative, seeing no trace
Of Lebanon or Egypt or the Holy
Land. But other palms survive
Down by the shielded harbour, and for me,
Even here, the exotic fronds still wave
On the heart's high place bestowed by Weymouth.

Textures and odours of the soft south,
Alive in the faith, in the love that pardons,
Are immune from the masked alien prowler.
I shall taste no more of spirit's winter,
And memories of Sandsfoot in the slant
Of a crowned day's gold confirm the undying transplant.

Keswick Revisited

Icelandic, Scandinavian, pagan anyway,
Lava of legends encrusted the Lakeland fells.
They rasped the same blind savagery
Through the storms' mock-Pentecost in winter,
While the old tongue's faded sagas
Kindled in raw-life shepherd's or poet's doom.

I was never here in winter,
But, decades ago, I felt warning tremors
At Ambleside, Coniston, even Skiddaw.
Though romance had blossomed, it was uneasy:
Red rowan berries could turn sinister,
Trailing a tragic ballad;
Playful pressure of becks meant erosion,
A slipped foothold on worn stones.

Yet I clung to hope, here as on Adelaide's Hill
When we laughed at the pelting of sudden rain.
Windermere based my twisted legend –
A warrior healed by beauty, the mere feminine grace.

But I knew in my clear-eyed core
That I fought for a creed which annulled all legends
And fed the nuptial bond on a higher grace.
She sensed this, and the last cold precipice
Held only the tumbled memories.

Now I mount the wide lobby, enter the Keswick tent –
A new thing, mine in my wife's orbit.
This woman of faith leads me along rows of chairs
Where believers pour hymns (thousands of voices strong)
On primal and tourist Keswick.

After the devotions we shall stroll,
Past stalls and open-air tables,
Down to the lake. Her first confirming glimpse
Of a Derwentwater familiar to me
But hardly hallowed till now. The whole scene's purged
Of pagan threats and the pattern of lost footholds.

Festal Magnet

An unjolted glide across Europe
With sandwiches eaten above the Alps
And my air-sickness bag unused
When the bump came, the neat landing
On a Venice runway. Soon a water-taxi
Proved me non-queasy in the swell
Of the cool Adriatic, then the lap
Of a canal soothed me until I stepped,
Awed despite my luggage, on the hotel path.

My mind, too, was firm and detached
From the ill turns of local history.
Byron at San Lazzaro,
Guilt-haunted Faust among monks; old Radetsky,
Fevered and senile behind the Austrian guns;
The skulking ferment of Pound;
And the more common dramas of dagger and poison
In the noble palaces.

I did not climb through the cloud barrier
To track these dark phantoms, but to contact
The soil and climate in which my faith
First reached into poetry, rich with Italian colour
Through Browning's pen. My Cornish images
Of smoke, iron and gravel
Stirred later on my drab fate's level.

In Venice I feel again the dawn
Spread from Pippa's Asolo, Guercino's Fano,
Andrea's wistful twilit Fiesole,
Rogue Lippi's Florence, aglow with God,
And the Arezzo crest, Pompilia's vision
That showed my goal beyond the clay sickness.

St Mark's now sanctions them all; its great dome
Looks softened and friendly in a warm sea-mist.
My clues thrive, more daringly festal,
Confirmed in their own land.

Palazzo Rezzonico
(for Benedict and Lilah)

Was there ever, in medieval Italy,
A more incredible wizardry? This whim and whisk
Of Providence peeled a foreign fate,
Breaking the dull smeared chrysalis,
Teaching a trick of levitation,
Air-flight at seventy-one, till the unclayed body
Boarded a gondola at Venice.

Canal-veined city: its golden heart now beats
Congruous to my new destiny,
Naming the broad sea, the split channels
Unstained by fevers of cramped history.
I sense, in this enchantment,
Not Doges and Shylocks but the gain
Of a soul's voyage to the point furthest out
From its natural source and scent
And the landmarks of the home-taught brain.

Back in Cornwall, remote from these flowing streets,
My Bridge of Sighs was an unfenced plank
Above the clay-slime. I felt giddy,
But even in my hermit-bonds prepared to thank
God for what native wit called mirage.

I clung, by stubborn grace, to the alien
Glitter of the Browning pattern
Which closed here, noble and clean,
Near the reserved church, in a frescoed palace.

Wedding allegory on a ceiling
Spills clues to the room of homage,
High over the nodding gondolas
And the whispering water's affirmation
Of outreach, the ultimate glad bridge.

Late Honeymoon

She looks up at the golden winged lion
    Mellow in St Mark's Square,
And she knows that more than a sprouting myth
    Brought our dream solidly here.

Doves make my raised arm a loaded branch;
    Eager beaks peck seeds off my palm:
All's a flutter from shoulder to finger-tip –
    And she feasts through the seeds in a psalm.

There's song and laughter on the floating station
    And the wide quivering water-buses:
Italy's joy crowns an English faith
    Which no ponderous school discusses.

Evolving structures are not for me;
    My life means prison or palace –
The biting iron fetter or a banquet
    With full-tilt chandelier and chalice.

We have stepped where sullen feet once stumbled
    At the Doge's point of the canal,
But the dolorous way was reversed for our love –
    Jail first, then this honeymoon hall.

It's in our souls and it holds all Venice –
    Rialto market, gondola, arch,
Grove-dusked islet and soft lagoon,
    And the bell-blithe hive of the church.

San Lazzaro

Byron's isle! Odd contrasts:
Flighty palms and the warm suck of tides
Almost at the harsh door
Of the Armenian monastery
Where a printing-press, trapped and greased
On the penitents' dry floor,
Spins at times, in stolid irony,
Leaves of *Childe Harold*, bound for English tourists.

Cowled monks will labour, praying for the soul
Of the satyr-bard who lodged here
Without a mistress, wooed by a viceless peace.
But I stood in his bedroom and felt nothing
Except that this was not my Venice.

Give me the Doges' symbol, the marriage-ring
Cast with the grave exultant ritual
Into the Adriatic. She is still wedded,
My rich city, to the sanctioned tongued sea.
I have thrilled to the ordered heaving
Near the nuptial fresco that drew Browning
From Camberwell, and now makes Weymouth palms
Part of the fertile answer
To the cold exile bed on San Lazzaro.

Venice

Italian skies, in a cold autumn,
Brood or sparkle above my hotel:
I sleep or sit with my wife at a table
While Southern light tones the canal close by,
And the carved laughing Arsenale lion.

The whole scene's a marvel, but it's abreast
Of my passport. I am not sucked back
From Heathrow hubbub to a stale serenade
Frail in an aesthetic glut. My legs ache
After climbing tiers of steps to bridge-tops
That take a road, unsoiled by petrol or tyres,
Through the perennial classic bounty.

Renaissance palaces and the bones
Of St Mark are not offended
By the modern canal transport, for that too
Moves within the spell. It carried me
To Rezzonico grandeur: a touch on a wall
Showed, still abreast, my literary lion,
Assured as the carved grin at the Arsenale,
And greeting the unseen as I shall do.

A Slant from St Mark's

Those Turkish domes, cool for six days,
Catch the sun's blaze at last. Crowds see the warm landmark,
Even from the distant hill-town, home
Of smouldering tarnished Ottima. But now
Someone shares the interior with me,
Probing Crusade spoil and the friendly
Legitimate splendour of jewels and carved stone.

We entered the incense cloud
By steps where sick pigeons fear the last chill,
And abruptly the scene spun personal meanings,
Ebb and rekindling of art within faith
Spelling my lifetime's changes.

I knew creative heat in Cornwall
As white glare on deformed sand, not domes,
Yet I found a shift while Europe smouldered,
Its culture tarnished and war-sick.

There it stood, the bland cathedral,
So unlike this one, sleek by the Kenwyn,
Delicate and modern, having no history
Of medieval romance. But as its spires
Twinkled I shaped my affirmation,
Probing nave and chancel,
Taking notes for my tale's end
Beyond clay, a flotsam love's arrival.

Ring and Pen

A Murano goblet, church wine for the Doge
After the sea-wedding. No signature
Marked the fluid bond, but centuries later
A betrothal pen struck an echo.
My partner gave me that pen
In the clay-waste of the sixties,
And it caught rich clues from Italy.

I confirmed those insights there
In the Doges' city of doves, bell-tongues
And holy running branches. The liquid criss-cross
Linked with Christ's cross in a safe ardour,
Chimes caressing the screened flow.

On balconies and water-buses,
In a stately gondola treading the Grand Canal,
Amid glass-factory heat, at café tables,
In Browning's death-room and by St Lucy's shrine,
I fingered the slim hard bulge
In my holiday coat. My faith's ripe outline,
Taking Venetian colour as she pressed me,
Made my heart swell, made the pen dearer,
Its labours vindicated.

Then a tremor of chill dismay
Struck our apartment on the first floor,
Tranquil scenes beyond the hotel window
Unheeded as we rummaged
Even under the bed, for my pocket was empty.

Tides bore the Doge's dropped ring
To the fish's mouth or the cliff crack –
A city's emblem, never cast astray.
But my recorder, our engagement trophy...

The tension ebbed. In a crevice
Near the window-frame, gold glinted suddenly.
My pen had lodged there, forced by thud and roll
None noticed amid the chatter, the glow
Of Rialto shopping. The lovers' pledge
Was usable again, and our voyaging joy
Relaxed in a whim of weather.

October rain had just pricked down
Where the Doge landed, at Porto di Lido,
And she had tripped through a Cornish deluge,
Bearing the pen, on our betrothal day.